CHICKENS
ON THE FAMILY FARM

Chana Stiefel

Enslow Elementary
an imprint of
Enslow Publishers, Inc.

40 Industrial Road
Box 398
Berkeley Heights, NJ 07922
USA
http://www.enslow.com

CONTENTS

WORDS TO KNOW

breed—A certain type of animal.

chick—A young chicken.

coop—A shelter for chickens.

down—Soft, fluffy feathers.

hen—A female chicken.

rooster—A male chicken.

PARTS OF A HEN

PARTS OF A ROOSTER

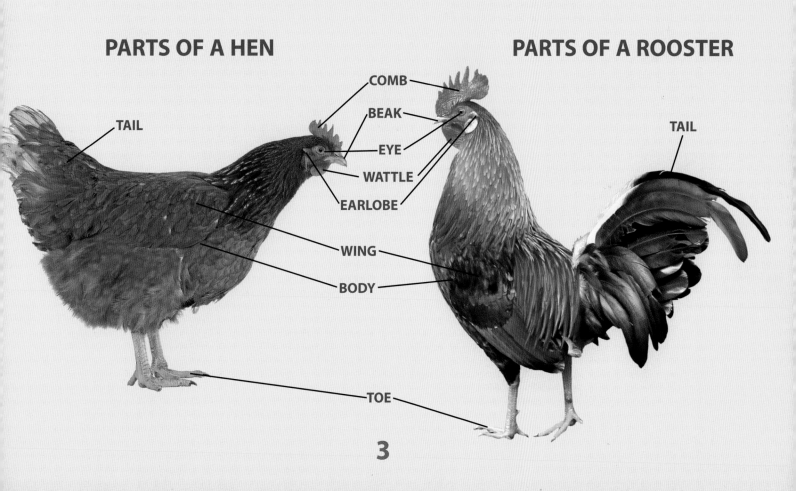

TAIL

COMB

BEAK

EYE

WATTLE

EARLOBE

TAIL

WING

BODY

TOE

3

These eggs aren't dyed. Some chickens lay colored eggs!

RAINBOW EGGS

Did you know that some chickens lay blue, green, or tan eggs? Find out more fun facts about chickens that live on the family farm.

"COCK-A-DOODLE-DOO!"

Tara (with Alice in front), Matt, and Jack are ready for the day.

The **roosters** are crowing. The sun is rising. It's time to wake up on the family farm. Farmers Matt and Tara go to the **coop** to feed the chickens. Their children, Jack and Alice, help out too.

6

Matt and Tara raise 150 hens that lay eggs. Another 1,000 chickens are raised for meat.

CHICKEN FEED

The farmers give the chickens grain to eat. The chickens roam in the fields and bushes, too. They eat wild grass and plants. They also love to eat bugs! The chickens peck at food all day. They come back to the coop to rest at night.

Chickens enjoy some flowers. Alice picks wild plants for the chickens to eat, too!

THE CHICKEN COOP

The coop looks like a big tent.
It is on wheels. Each day, the farmers roll
the coop down the field. This way, the
chickens always find fresh grass to eat.

When the weather is bad, the chickens go inside the coop. Alice likes to watch the chickens.

This rooster makes lots of noise to warn the chickens of danger.

WATCH OUT!

A hungry fox is coming!
The roosters protect the **hens**.
They squawk. They flap their
wings. The chickens run into
the coop. They are safe there.

Foxes, hawks, and owls like to hunt for chickens.
The roosters watch out for these animals.

NESTING
TIME

Hens lay their eggs in a nest.

Inside the coop, the hens sit on their nests. They lay eggs every day or two. Different **breeds** lay eggs with different colors. Jack gently puts the eggs in a basket. On some days, Jack collects 150 eggs!

Different breeds of chickens are different colors.

"PEEP, PEEP!"
CHICKS
HATCH

Baby **chicks** are tiny. You can hold one in your hand. The farmers use heat lamps to keep them warm. The chicks stay in a warm area for a few months. They eat lots of grain. They drink milk.

People come to the barn at Matt and Tara's farm to buy fresh, healthy food.

FRESH
FOOD

Some chickens are raised for meat. People come to the farm to pick up fresh chickens to cook and eat. They take home eggs, too. They also buy fruits and vegetables for a healthy meal.

Matt and Tara sell farm fresh eggs.

MANY DIFFERENT
CHICKENS

Not all chickens are the same. There are different breeds. Some are good for laying eggs. Others are raised for meat. See how different they look? Which is your favorite?

Wyandotte,
eggs and meat

Barred Rock,
eggs and meat

Buff Orpington,
eggs and meat

20

Ameraucana, eggs

Black Australorp, eggs

Cochin, meat

Pekin Cochin, meat

LIFE CYCLE OF A CHICKEN

1. A hen sits on her eggs for about 21 days. She keeps them warm. Crack! The eggs hatch!

2. The chicks are covered with soft, fluffy **down**. They slowly grow new feathers. By four weeks, all of their feathers are fully grown.

3. By 18 weeks, hens start to lay eggs. Chickens may live five to six years.

LEARN MORE

BOOKS

Ganeri, Anita. *From Egg to Chicken*. Mankato, Minn.: Heinemann-Raintree, 2005.

Macken, JoAnn Early. *Chickens*. Pleasantville, N.Y.: Weekly Reader, 2010.

Ray, Hannah. *Chickens*. New York: Crabtree Pub. Co., 2008.

WEB SITES

Kids Farm.
<http://www.kidsfarm.com/farm.htm>

Smithsonian National Zoological Park. *Kids' Farm.*
http://www.nationalzoo.si.edu/Animals/KidsFarm/IntheBarn

INDEX

Enslow Elementary, an imprint of Enslow Publishers, Inc.
Enslow Elementary® is a registered trademark of Enslow Publishers, Inc.

Copyright © 2013 by Chana Stiefel

Library of Congress Cataloging-in-Publication Data

Stiefel, Chana, 1968-
Chickens on the family farm / Chana Stiefel.
    p. cm. — (Animals on the family farm)
  Summary: "An introduction to life on a farm for early readers. Find out what a chicken eats, where it lives, and its life cycle from baby chick to adult."—Provided by publisher.
Includes index.
  ISBN 978-0-7660-4204-9
1. Chickens—Juvenile literature. I. Title. II. Series: Animals on the family farm.
SF487.5.S74 2013
636.5—dc23
                    2012028800

Future editions:
Paperback ISBN: 978-1-4644-0351-4
EPUB ISBN: 978-1-4645-1194-3
Single-User PDF ISBN: 978-1-4646-1194-0
Multi-User PDF ISBN: 978-0-7660-5826-2

Printed in China

012013 Leo Paper Group, Heshan City, Guangdong, China

10 9 8 7 6 5 4 3 2 1

To Our Readers: We have done our best to make sure all Internet Addresses in this book were active and appropriate when we went to press. However, the author and the publisher have no control over and assume no liability for the material available on those Internet sites or on other Web sites they may link to. Any comments or suggestions can be sent by e-mail to comments@enslow.com or to the address on the back cover.

Photo Credits: Photos.com: Christine Nichols, p. 20 (Wyandotte), Craig Veltri, p. 17, Edward Ralph, p. 21 (Black Australorp, Cochin), Mark Balyshev, p. 14, Petrus van der Westhuizen, p. 15, Studio-Annika, p. 22 (egg), Thinkstock Images, pp. 4–5, Valorie Webster, p. 19, Weldon Schloneger, p. 8.; Howling Wolf Farm, pp. 6, 11, 18; © iStockphoto.com/Iain Sarjeant, p. 22 (chicken); Shutterstock.com, pp. 1, 2, 3, 7, 9, 12, 13, 16, 20 (Barred Rock, Buff Orpington), 21 (Ameraucana, Pekin Cochin), 22 (chick);

Cover Photograph: Shutterstock.com

A note from Matt and Tara of Howling Wolf Farm: Howling Wolf Farm grows vital food to feed individuals and families. Products include vegetables, dry beans and grains, dairy, beef, eggs, chicken, lamb, and pork. We work in partnership with nature and people to grow vibrant, abundant food. We farm with an intention of creating a farm and food to bring health, vitality, and enjoyment to our complete beings and the land. We focus on heirloom and open-pollinated varieties, heritage breeds, and wild foods.

Series Science Consultant:
Dana Palmer
Sr. Extension Associate/4-H Youth Outreach
Department of Animal Science
Cornell University
Ithaca, NY

Series Literacy Consultant:
Allan A. De Fina, Ph.D.
Past President of the New Jersey
    Reading Association
Dean of the College of Education
New Jersey City University
Jersey City, NJ